SUPER FEMALE SCIENTISTS™

MAE JEMISON

FIRST FEMALE AFRICAN AMERICAN ASTRONAUT

Xina M. Uhl and Magdalena Alagna

Rosen YA™
New York

Published in 2020 by The Rosen Publishing Group, Inc.
29 East 21st Street, New York, NY 10010

First Edition

Library of Congress Cataloging-in-Publication Data

Names: Uhl, Xina M., author. | Alagna, Magdalena, author.
Title: Mae Jemison : first female African American astronaut / Xina M. Uhl and Magdalena Alagna.
Description: First edition. | New York : Rosen Publishing, 2020 | Series: Super female scientists | Audience: Grades 7–12. | Includes bibliographical references and index.
Identifiers: LCCN 2019007262| ISBN 9781725340480 (library bound) | ISBN 9781725340473 (pbk.)
Subjects: LCSH: Jemison, Mae, 1956- —Juvenile literature. | African American women astronauts—Biography—Juvenile literature. | Astronauts—United States—Biography—Juvenile literature. | African American women—Biography—Juvenile literature.
Classification: LCC TL789.85.J46 U45 2020 | DDC 629.45/0092 [B]—dc23
LC record available at https://lccn.loc.gov/2019007262

Manufactured in the United States of America

On the cover: Astronaut Mae Jemison, floating weightless inside a spacecraft, joined NASA in 1987, flew on the space shuttle in 1992, and resigned from NASA the following year.

CONTENTS

INTRODUCTION

When Mae Jemison was five years old, a teacher asked her what she wanted to be when she grew up. Young Mae, who had become interested in science the previous year, promptly replied that she wanted to be a scientist, to the teacher's astonishment. It wouldn't be the only time that Mae astonished others.

Throughout her childhood, Mae learned about scientific subjects that fascinated and delighted her: anthropology, archaeology, and astronomy. Her sharp intellect allowed her to skip the seventh grade entirely. She graduated from high school at sixteen years old. Mae then entered Stanford University in California on a National Achievement Scholarship. Mae went on to accomplish her childhood goal, and more, without stopping to dwell on the obstacles that had almost blocked her path.

As she was growing up, Mae had a clear vision of what she wanted to accomplish in her life. She wanted to achieve a variety of goals and to use her knowledge to help others. Following her interests, Jemison graduated from Stanford in 1977 with a dual degree in chemical engineering and Afro-American studies. She went on to medical school at Cornell University and received a doctor of medicine degree in 1981.

STS-47 Mission Specialist Mae C. Jemison poses for her official astronaut photo for the fiftieth space shuttle misssion of the entire program (but only space shuttle *Endeavour*'s second mission).

As a medical volunteer in a Cambodian refugee camp and a member and medical officer with the Peace Corps, she served patients in West Africa. While in Africa, Jemison worked with the Centers for Disease Control and Prevention (CDC) and the National Institutes of Health (NIH) on several research projects, including the development of a hepatitis B vaccine. Much of her time has been devoted to working with children. She developed a science camp for teens, and in other projects she worked to make school science and technology classes easier to understand.

Her work took her to Los Angeles, where she became a general medical practitioner. From there, she and fourteen others were selected by the National Aeronautics and Space Administration (NASA) for astronaut training.

With her training as a mission specialist with NASA completed in 1988, she became an astronaut. In 1992, she became a mission specialist aboard the space shuttle *Endeavour*, to become the first African American woman to enter space. It is for this feat that Jemison is most known.

But Jemison was not through achieving her goals by a long shot. After her 1993 resignation from NASA, she founded the Jemison Group, Inc. The group's projects involved initiatives to improve health care in Africa and working in developing countries to advance technology.

Mae Jemison has accomplished incredible feats. In addition to becoming the first black female astronaut, she worked as a doctor, a scientist, and a teacher. As if that wasn't enough, she made time to learn to speak Japanese, Swahili, and Russian fluently. She also serves on the board of directors for several corporations and helps others by organizing a science camp called The Earth We Share (TEWS).

Jemison has been able to accomplish an incredible amount in her lifetime. How? Her book of collected interviews, lectures, and autobiography, *Find Where the Wind Goes: Moments from My Life*, reveals that she did it by staying true to herself and her goals rather than allowing herself to dwell on obstacles and setbacks.

CHAPTER ONE

A LOVE OF SCIENCE

On October 17, 1956, in Decatur, Alabama, Mae Carol Jemison, the youngest of three children, was born to Charlie and Dorothy Jemison. Her father worked as a maintenance supervisor. Her mother became a teacher. Her siblings include a sister, Ada Sue, and a brother, Charles, whose nickname is Ricky. In her autobiography, Jemison lists her own nicknames. At the hospital after her birth, the nurses called her Rosebud because of the shape of her lips. Her father called her Fattening Bug because she grew so quickly as a toddler.

Though she essentially grew up in Chicago, Illinois, far from Decatur, where she was born, Mae

Mae Jemison's birthplace, Decatur, Alabama, is located on the Tennessee River. Shown here are early and late twentieth century buildings on Bank Street, the city's downtown district.

would visit Alabama on occasion. Decatur is near Huntsville, Alabama, home of the Marshall Space Flight Center, and Mae would eventually spend much time there during her astronaut training.

According to her autobiography, Jemison has fond memories of Decatur. Among these memories is a shocking story of how she, as a two-year-old, drove her father's car. As the story goes, Dorothy and Charlie Jemison and some of their friends had gone shopping with little Mae. They pulled into the parking lot of a store, and Dorothy got out to pick up some groceries. She needed help carrying the bags, so Charlie got out of the car to help her. Mae, right under the noses of Charlie's two friends, clambered into the front seat of Charlie's Buick and managed to pop the clutch, put the car in gear, and hit the gas pedal. However, she was too little to see over the steering wheel, and the car quickly smashed into three parked cars.

The Windy City

When Mae was three years old, the family moved to Chicago. In her autobiography, Jemison wrote that her mother decided to move to Chicago because there weren't as many opportunities for work in Decatur, Alabama. In fact, Jemison recalled visiting Decatur as an adult, and she admitted that it was a sleepy little town. In Decatur at that time, most black women could find work only as maids for white people. Dorothy Jemison had gone to college for two years at Talladega College in Alabama, and she wanted to complete her bachelor's degree. She packed up her three children and moved to Chicago. Charlie Jemison, who had not at first wanted to leave Alabama, followed a few months later. Dorothy did, in fact, finish her degree and became a schoolteacher. She also went on to get her master's degree. Mae's mom served as a good role model for the young girl. Mae learned early on that a good education was very important.

At first, the Jemisons lived in the Woodlawn section of Chicago. Mae Jemison remembers being afraid of the dark and that her brother and sister would lock her in the basement of their house, with all the lights turned out. Mae Jemison was a self-described "scaredy-cat" who was not only afraid of the dark but also afraid of heights. As a girl, Mae wanted to take dance lessons, but to get to the dance studio she would have to take the "L." The "L" (for "elevated") is the train in Chicago that rides above the ground, unlike the subway trains in other cities. Mae didn't dare look down while she was waiting on the train platform. She said that she outgrew her fear of heights when her natural curiosity and love of dancing got the better of her fear. In the face of her overwhelming need to know, all fear was forgotten.

A Woman's Place Is in the Lab

When Mae Jemison was five years old, she had an experience in kindergarten at Woodlawn Elementary School that illustrates a lot about her drive to succeed. According to her autobiography, Mae's teacher asked the students what they wanted to be when they grew up. Many of the students said things like police officer, mail carrier, or firefighter. When the teacher called on Mae, she answered loud and clear, "I want to be a scientist." The teacher looked a little confused. It was 1961, and there were not that many opportunities in science for women, not to mention black women. "Don't you mean a nurse?" the teacher asked. "No, I mean a scientist," she said again, making sure that there could be no misunderstanding.

When Mae's older brother, Ricky, was threatened by a gang member in front of the Jemison house, Dorothy Jemison insisted that the family move out of Woodlawn and into Morgan Park. There was a lot of gang activity in Woodlawn, but there was not as much in Morgan Park. Mae was ten years old when the family moved into Morgan Park, where her family was the first black family on the block. Her teacher from her last school had requested that Mae be allowed to skip the seventh grade and go right into eighth grade because she was able to do eighth-grade work.

Studying and Studying Some More

One of the first science experiments Mae Jemison did was called Eras of Time. It was a study of the evolution of the universe. Mae worked on the project from third until sixth grade. Each year, she spent time after school and during the summers at the library, where she would research different eras of time, such as the Mesozoic era, the time when the dinosaurs lived. She constructed dioramas of each era of time. In the fifth and sixth grades, she came across the work of Harold Urey and Stanley L. Miller, scientists who worked to understand how life formed on Earth. Urey and Miller's research sparked the girl's curiosity and imagination. Mae loved piecing together the clues of human evolution using information provided in the research of prominent scientists. Mae also read many books about dinosaurs.

Everyone in the Jemison family had a library card, and visits to the library were a big part of Mae Jemison's childhood. Dorothy and Charlie Jemison encouraged all of their children to learn. It was during this time that Mae also became fascinated with astronomy, the study of things outside our

The Adler Planetarium in Chicago was one of Mae's favorite places to visit while growing up. The planetarium, the first in the Western Hemisphere, opened in 1930.

atmosphere. She often went to Chicago's Adler Planetarium. It was her love of astronomy that brought her to read Fred Hoyle's books.

Fred Hoyle was a British astronomer. He also wrote science fiction novels, such as *A for Andromeda*. After Mae read this novel, she couldn't get enough of science fiction books. She also liked the authors Isaac Asimov and Arthur C. Clarke, as well as Madeleine L'Engle's *A Wrinkle in Time* and *The Arm of the Starfish*. She especially liked Madeleine L'Engle's books because they featured women scientists as heroines. However, in her autobiography, Mae wrote that she also identified with the white male heroes of Asimov's and Clarke's books. Mystery and adventure were what allowed her to identify with these characters. In science fiction, the characters often go on mysterious adventures. Mae also felt that life was a mysterious adventure.

The Liberal Arts

Dorothy and Charlie Jemison always talked about politics and social science with their children, as did their uncle Louis, Charlie's brother. The Jemison children were interested in black history and in

Miriam Makeba performs in a show that also featured Harry Belafonte in Toronto, Canada, on July 3, 1967. She danced and sang an Israeli ballad and a protest song.

figures such as Paul Robeson, an athlete, singer, actor, and activist. At a time when African Americans were encountering a lot of racial prejudice that kept them from pursuing meaningful careers, Paul Robeson was successful in his chosen career. He was an all-American football player at Rutgers University, and he went on to appear in plays such as *Othello* and also in several films, such as *Showboat*. The family was also influenced by South African singer Miriam Makeba. After seeing her in concert, Dorothy was struck by the singer's natural hairstyle. In the 1960s, many black women were using chemicals to straighten their hair so that it could be styled much the way a white person's hair is styled. However, Makeba wore her hair short and naturally curly. Dorothy decided that she and her girls would wear their hair the same way. For Mae Jemison, this was a good introduction to the civil rights movement that was starting to take hold in the 1960s.

The civil rights movement in America was spearheaded by groups such as the NAACP (National Association for the Advancement of Colored People) and by Martin Luther King Jr. in the 1950s and 1960s. The movement raised national awareness in America about the way blacks were treated, and it resulted in the Civil Rights Act of 1964, which made discrimination against people based on their color, race, or religion against the law. Malcolm X and Stokely Carmichael, two important figures in the civil rights movement, were often discussed in the Jemison household. Malcolm X was a militant black leader who was assassinated in 1965. Stokely Carmichael, a prominent figure in the civil rights movement, chanted the phrase "Black is Beautiful" at a student rally in 1965.

Riots occurred across the United States during the summers of the mid-1960s. In the summer of 1968, Mae Jemison was twelve years old. It was the year that Martin Luther King Jr., an important leader in the civil rights movement, was shot, and Mae Jemison remembers cowering in her house in Chicago while a riot was going on. Running to the front window, she peeped outside and saw crowds of people on the street, among which were the National Guard. Mae was scared, even though some of the National Guardsmen were black. Children had been killed during the riots, and Mae did not trust that the soldiers would protect her. Then she reminded herself that she was just as much a part of the United States as the soldiers were. It was a scary but ultimately empowering experience for the young girl. She never forgot that everyone must contribute to making the world a better place and that each person must do his or her part for peace, knowledge, and understanding.

Jemison's Creative Side

Mae Jemison entered high school when she was just twelve years old. She was tall for her age, already about 5 feet 6 inches (168 centimeters) of what would eventually be her full height of 5 feet 9 inches (175 cm). She was not intimidated by all the older kids because of her height and also because she wanted to study so badly. In high school, she had the opportunity to study physics, chemistry, and biology. She also continued dancing, and she tried out for cheerleading and school plays. There was so much to do in high school that she didn't have time to be intimidated as one of the youngest first-year students. During her senior year, she was even the student council president.

Mae studied Russian throughout her four years of high school. She was convinced that Russian would be an important language to know when she was working in the scientific community. Surprisingly, Mae got a D in gym class during her first semester in high school. Mae had a hard time keeping her gym shoes polished brightly enough to satisfy her gym teacher. This D in gym was a good lesson in humility for the confident young girl. Another lesson was trying out for the school production of *West Side Story*. Although Mae was a good dancer, she couldn't sing a note. She decided to try out anyway, but when the director heard her sing, she had to kiss the star part she wanted goodbye. Instead, Mae was given a part in the chorus.

When she was fifteen, Mae worked at Cook County Hospital, in the hematology lab. (Hematology is the study of the blood.) Mae was hired to do research for a project about sickle-cell anemia, a deadly disease that mainly affects African Americans. It was during this project that Mae began to understand that she not only had to run experiments and collect data. If she wanted to be a scientist, she would have to come up with hypotheses to test. This was a big step for the young girl who initially hadn't even wanted to call the hematology lab to ask whether she would be allowed to work

A visiting nurse attends to a patient's leg ulcer. Sickle cell anemia, which causes ulcers and other problems, affects African Americans more than other racial groups.

on her project there. She understood what learning experiences she could have if she just persevered in spite of her initial fear.

With all of her science projects and student council work, it would seem that Mae didn't have much time for fun. But high school was not all work and no play. Mae spent time with friends and even dated a little, although she was not technically allowed to go out on dates until she was sixteen. She also had time to engage in a few good pranks with her brother and sister. Once she dumped a bucket of ice water on her brother when he was asleep!

At sixteen years old, Mae Jemison was ready for her next adventure. She would be going to college at Stanford University in California.

CHAPTER TWO

THE COLLEGE YEARS

Wearing homemade clothes, sixteen-year-old Mae Jemison boarded a plane to California filled with excitement, and some fear. She had never been to California, but she was headed to Stanford University with the help of a National Achievement Scholarship.

Mae got scholarship offers from all of the schools to which she applied, including the Massachusetts Institute of Technology, Cornell University, and Rensselaer Polytechnic Institute, but there were a few reasons why she chose Stanford University. Stanford had famous scientists such as Dr. Linus Pauling on the faculty. Pauling was the only person

This yearbook photo from Morgan Park High School shows Mae Jemison during the time she attended school there.

in the world to have won two unshared Nobel Prizes, one in 1954 for chemistry and one in 1962 for peace, for trying to stop the atmospheric testing of nuclear weapons. Stanford had radio telescopes on campus, great engineering and medical programs, and the Stanford Linear Accelerator Center (SLAC). The SLAC is a national laboratory operated by Stanford University for the US Department of Energy. It is a famous research center that does important and high-profile work.

Stanford also had a great football team. Mae was (and still is) a self-described football fanatic. At Stanford she would not only watch football, she also played in the coed intramural football leagues. Stanford also was a place of much political activism and social awareness. It was the first school to have coeducational dormitories with female and male students living on the same floor. That was a big deal at the time, and magazine articles were written about it.

Race and Obstacles

When she got to Stanford, Mae planned to major in biomedical engineering, and she was confident that she was prepared for that area of study. Biomedical engineering is a scientific discipline in which the principles of mathematics, science, and medicine are applied to the study of technology. However, it wasn't clear to her whether biomedical engineering at Stanford University was ready for her. When she met her adviser during a student orientation event held at his house, Mae was struck by the fact that she was not only one of the few women there, she was the only black person there. People seemed to be friendly to each other, but they didn't talk to her much, not even when she tried to join in the conversation. She had gone to an integrated high school, where there were students of many different races and ethnic backgrounds. She had been the student council president, and she was not used to being overlooked either academically or socially. At Stanford, it appeared that she would be judged by her appearance, her gender, and the color of her skin. Although she had sometimes disagreed with her teachers in high school, they had never doubted that she was capable of doing well academically. It would take her a while to find her way at Stanford.

During her first semester, she took calculus, solid analytic geometry, introductory chemistry, a freshman seminar on women's physiology, a freshman English class focused on African American literature, and tennis. She was especially excited about chemistry because it had been one of her favorite subjects in high school. However, her professor turned out to be every bit as difficult as she had been warned that he was. Mae sat in the front row of the lecture hall and participated in class, asking questions. She was excited because she was learning about things that interested her. But the professor would either ignore her questions or make her feel stupid for having asked them. When a white male student asked the same questions, however, the teacher would praise him for his insight. Mae finally took the not-so-subtle hint and stopped asking questions.

Switching Directions

Mae got a new adviser during the second quarter of her freshman year. Mae first had become aware of biomedical engineering as a profession during a two-week program that she attended during the summer before her senior year in high school. Scientists at the University of Illinois showed the students how to perform lab experiments in biomedical engineering. Biomedical engineers are scientists who develop artificial organs and limbs. They also deal with tissue regeneration and develop bionic body parts like computer-operated hands for people who've lost their hands in accidents. One example of a device developed by biomedical engineers is the pacemaker. It is a machine that is implanted in a person's chest to regulate the rhythm of his or her heart. Mae was attracted to biomedical engineering because she loved science and was good at many different branches of it. This was a field that required a knowledge of many different scientific fields, including chemistry, biology, and physics.

But Mae's new adviser believed she should get a degree in chemical engineering, instead of biomedical engineering. Chemical engineering is a science that applies the principles of chemistry, the study of substances, to engineering, which is the designing and making of products that are useful to people. He advised her to do that because biomedical engineering was a new field at that time, and its course of study was not fixed—it was sort of like designing your own major. If she took chemical engineering, everyone would know that she had gone through a rigorous program and had gotten a classical science degree. Not only that, but chemical engineering required most, if not all, of the same

Russian or Swahili?

Because the Jemisons had always encouraged their children to be well-rounded, Mae wanted to take some language courses at Stanford. She had taken four years of Russian in high school and was convinced that speaking Russian was an important qualification for a scientist to have. Why didn't she take Russian at Stanford? She had asked her first adviser how to figure out which courses she should take in the Russian language, and he had told her that if the Russian language department had not contacted her she should just assume she should take beginning Russian. Mae was embarrassed that she might not have done well enough on her placement exams to take a more advanced Russian course, even after studying it for four years in high school. She was so embarrassed that she did not even go to the Russian department to inquire what her score was. She took Swahili instead, partly because she thought she would like it, and partly because her older sister, Ada Sue, had taken Swahili in college. This was not the only African course that she took during her first year.

courses that a degree in biomedical engineering would have, plus a few more.

Although she would later live in Roble Hall, where many African American students lived, she

The Black Student Union at Stanford University conducts a protest on campus. In the 1970s, this student organization was on the forefront of calls for racial equality.

did not start out there. She was living at the Alondra House and was the youngest person in the dorm. This at times led to funny situations, such as when Mae got a traffic ticket and had to take someone in the dorm, someone older than eighteen years of age, with her to traffic court. Mae made friends in her dorm that were to last a lifetime. One friend from Alondra House, Linda Jones, years later became an anchor on the Houston, Texas, evening news, and she covered Mae's launch into space.

Cultural Pursuits

During her sophomore year, Mae took a political science class called Politics in Sub-Saharan Africa. She also took African dance courses.

She became the president of the Black Student Union, an organization that represented the black students on campus. This representation included providing a place where black students could voice their concerns and where they could be sure of gaining help to address those concerns. The Black Student Union also was a social organization where people could make friends. Mae designed and helped to teach a class called Race and Politics in Education

African dance performances like the one shown here incorporate traditional instruments, costumes, and music in stunning displays.

and one called Race and Culture in the Caribbean. She continued to take classes in Swahili and African history, culture, and politics. During the fall of her senior year, she found she needed just two required courses to get a bachelor of arts degree in African and Afro-American studies. Chemical engineering had the most required courses of any field of study at Stanford. Mae was also juggling extracurricular activities and a social life. How and why did she find time to complete all of the requirements for a bachelor of arts degree in African studies?

Jemison recalled in her autobiography that the professors in the African studies department welcomed her into their classes and wanted her there. Their attitude was a welcome change from that of many of her chemical engineering professors, who did not give her any indication that they believed in her ability to do the work. Mae believes that she was unconsciously balancing the poor reception that she got in the science classes with the positive reception she got in the social sciences.

Those She Looked Up To

Jemison graduated from Stanford University with a bachelor of science degree in chemical engineering and qualified for a bachelor of arts degree in African and Afro-American studies. Throughout her college experience, Jemison had some role models who helped her to remember all that she was striving to accomplish. These role models were people who were making a difference in the world. For instance,

Gloria Steinem was a leader of the feminist movement of the 1970s, demanding better pay, working conditions, and a focus on women's issues.

Gloria Steinem, a now-famous feminist, was at that time a journalist who brought to the public's attention how women were thought of in our culture and what need there was for feminism and radical change in people's attitudes toward women. Jemison studied Julius Nyerere, the president of Tanzania, a country in East Africa. She was fascinated with how Nyerere worked to keep Tanzania free of the politics of both the Soviet Union and the United States. It was not an easy thing for a small country to avoid the influences of two such powerful countries, and Jemison saw in Nyerere's leadership a way to navigate her own life, taking from the strong what she needed to survive, but without compromising herself.

However inspirational these people were for Jemison, she cites as her real role models the people she knew growing up—the members of her family and her teachers. It was from them that she learned the importance of knowledge, of applying knowledge, and of being well-rounded and self-reliant. Her uncle Louis was the one who had introduced her to Albert Einstein's theory of relativity. Her aunt Melvyn, who worked at a dry cleaner's, took Jemison to work with her and taught her about the importance of working hard and doing a job well and with pride.

Her brother and sister taught her how to play chess. Her father taught her how to play a game called bid whist, which is similar to the card game bridge.

Stanford University had been an eye-opening experience for the smart, ambitious young woman. However, she wrote in her autobiography that she did not really learn how to study until she reached medical school. It was there that she would discover that, no matter how smart you were, there was no escaping studying every day, after having been in class from nine to five!

CHAPTER THREE

DR. JEMISON

After a summer in San Jose as an engineer with IBM, Mae Jemison headed to the East Coast—specifically, New York City. At just twenty years old, she was enrolling in medical school at Cornell University Medical College (CUMC), one of the United States' best medical schools.

Though Jemison brought a solid scientific background with her, she did not really consider herself a premed student. She did not intend to practice medicine. She was taking a degree in medicine to pursue her goal of working in biomedical engineering. What really attracted Jemison to medical school was applying scientific and medical technology to help people and better their quality of life. Therefore, when she met her new roommate and saw her sprawled over a desk spread with textbooks, Jemison was confused.

Classes didn't start for two days. She hadn't even gotten her textbooks yet, and her roommate had already begun studying!

Luckily for Jemison, the students got together to play bid whist to get to know each other before classes started. This was the card game that her father had taught her how to play. Jemison showed her feminist streak by helping the women's bid whist team to win when they competed against the men.

Medical school did not have a big, organized orientation session like they had had at college. The students got their schedules and the information about the physical exams and vaccinations that they needed. But none of this prepared Jemison for gross anatomy class. It was in this class that students learned about muscles, internal organs, blood vessels, bones, and nerves. They learned all this by dissecting a human body. A dissecting manual was one of the books that Jemison's roommate had been studying just days before. Jemison, however, had never done anything that could have prepared her to dissect a human cadaver. There wasn't even a lecture first. The students put on their lab coats and went into the lab to dissect. It was during this time that Jemison realized that she had better start studying

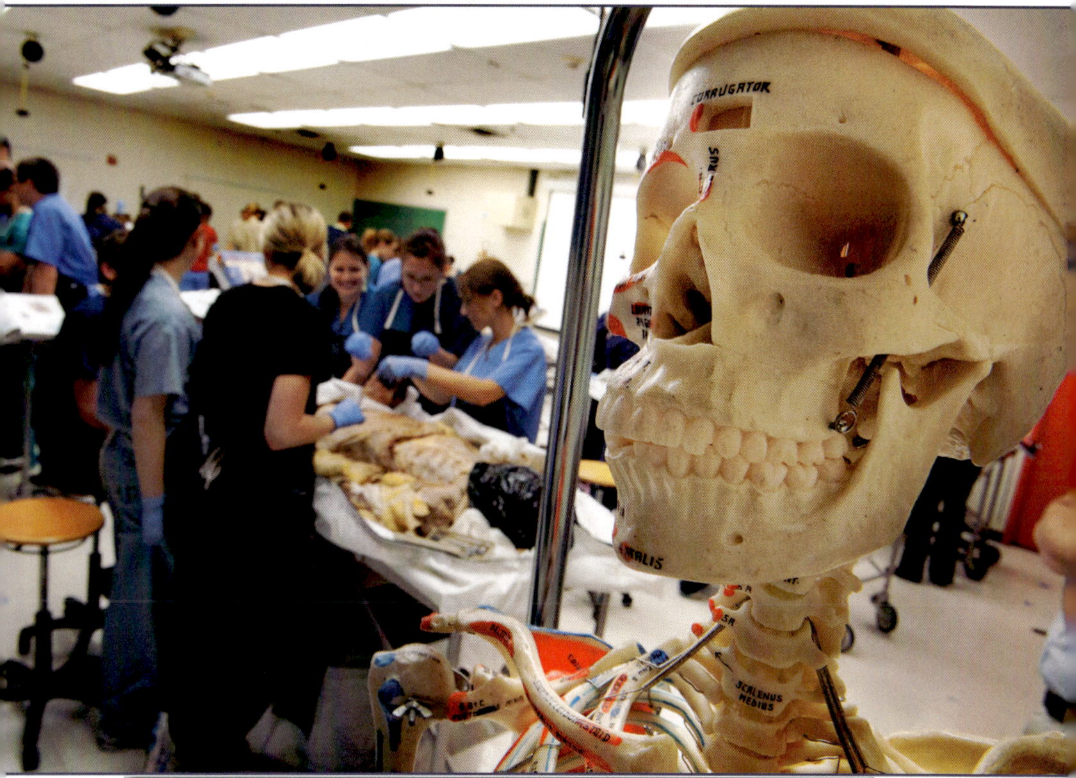

Medical students, like these at Georgetown University in Washington, DC, rely on donated cadavers to learn about human anatomy.

hard. She was almost totally lost during that first gross anatomy class. She was, however, proud of herself for conquering her fear and actually touching an exposed muscle.

It took her about two weeks to learn the medical vocabulary she needed to feel comfortable dissecting cadavers in gross anatomy lab. As for her other classes, at first Jemison thought that her roommate and friends were going a little overboard by concentrating on memorizing details such as the names of minor blood vessels. They made a game out of it, giving each other pop quizzes and challenging each other to get the right answers. Sometimes they even sneaked into the gross anatomy lab at night to go over what they had done that day and to imprint it in their memories. Jemison didn't do anything of the kind. She thought that it would be enough for the students to understand the mechanics of the body and how everything works. One day, she asked her teacher during a lecture on an artery abnormality if they were expected to remember even the smallest details. After staring at her hard for a moment, he explained that she would, in fact, need to pay attention to such details.

Although she had studied in the afternoons at Stanford, she was not used to pulling all-nighters, doing so only twice in her undergraduate career. When she got to medical school, it was common for her to study until two o'clock in the morning. In her autobiography, Jemison recounted the experience of being so engrossed in her classwork that she would meet new people and imagine seeing their body parts. She imagined what it would be like if a person she was talking to was accidentally hit with a spear during the conversation. Which structures of the body would she be able to see? Which would be damaged, depending on the angle that the spear hit? These were the same as many of the questions asked in gross anatomy exams.

The Legendary Katherine Dunham

Born in Chicago in 1909, Katherine Dunham had an African American father and a French Canadian mother. As a child, she sang in her local church but never thought of a career in show business, instead attending the University of Chicago and earning a bachelor's degree, a master's degree, and a PhD in anthropology—one of a very few number of African American women to do so at the time.

Dunham's background in anthropology took her on field studies in Brazil and the Caribbean, where she

(continued on p. 43)

Katherine Dunham performs with her Tropical Review in 1944. An anonymous review published in the *Harvard Crimson* called the show "a fine array of hot music."

(continued from p. 41)

studied dance rituals. Back in the United States, she revolutionized dance in the 1930s by integrating what she had learned abroad when she founded an all-black dance company. She toured the country and became involved in Broadway stage productions and dance numbers for Hollywood films.

Human rights issues also interested her, and she staged a hunger strike forty-seven days in 1992 to bring attention to the difficult conditions experienced by Haitian refugees.

She died in 2006 at ninety-seven years of age.

Social Activities

Jemison continued to take African dance classes. In New York, she studied with Katherine Dunham, a well-known dancer who was renowned for her techniques. Jemison's roommate, Joan, also taught her how to play pool. The young women also played basketball games in the gym at school. Many of the premed students played basketball to relax and blow off steam. The games were coed, and they could sometimes get aggressive.

Of course, Jemison enjoyed many of the delights of being in New York City. New York is home to the

Alvin Ailey dance troupe, a troupe of dancers that Jemison greatly admired. Not only did she take some classes at the Alvin Ailey dance studio, she went to see the troupe perform, as well as seeing the New York City Ballet and plays.

Drawing on her talent for performance, which she had not done since high school, Jemison wrote a funny sketch with her roommate, Joan. They and their friend Blaine performed the skit for the class Christmas show. It involved one of their stuffy professors becoming lost in Harlem and being propositioned by a woman on a street corner. The woman was Jemison herself, dressed in hot pants and high-heeled boots.

Some of the extracurricular activities that Jemison was involved in were purely for fun. Some happened to be fun but were also for the betterment of others. For instance, during her first year in medical school, Jemison helped to put together a publication for high school students about the dangers of prescription drug abuse. She did this with a friend, Rupa Redding. They went into the area high schools to distribute the publication and to talk to the students about prescription drug abuse. During her second year, she helped to put together a health and law fair with students at Columbia University Law School, and with medical students from New Jersey Medical and Dental, New York University, Cornell, and Columbia. At the time, she was the president of the Cornell chapter of the Student National Medical Association. During her third year, Jemison was elected president of the Cornell Student Executive Committee, and during her final year in medical school, she was Cornell's student representative to the Association of American Medical Colleges.

If dissection labs were a challenge in Jemison's first year in medical school, there was a surprise waiting for her during her second year, in the form of microbiology lab. In this lab, students would experiment with blood to understand how antibodies are produced as a result of vaccinations, such as the typhoid vaccination. There was just one little thing on which Jemison hadn't counted—the students would be supplying the blood for the experiments. Jemison recalled in her autobiography that her lab partner had a difficult time getting the blood from her arm and that, in fact, the professor had to do it. Also during her second year, Jemison took a class called physical diagnosis and was granted her medical instruments. The class taught students how to do the things doctors do during physical checkups, such as take blood pressure, listen to heartbeat and breathing, check reflexes, and examine the eyes and ears. "Owning a stethoscope meant you really were becoming a doctor," Jemison wrote in her autobiography. The instruments were expensive, so she skimped where she could. For instance, she didn't order the classic black doctor bag and used a

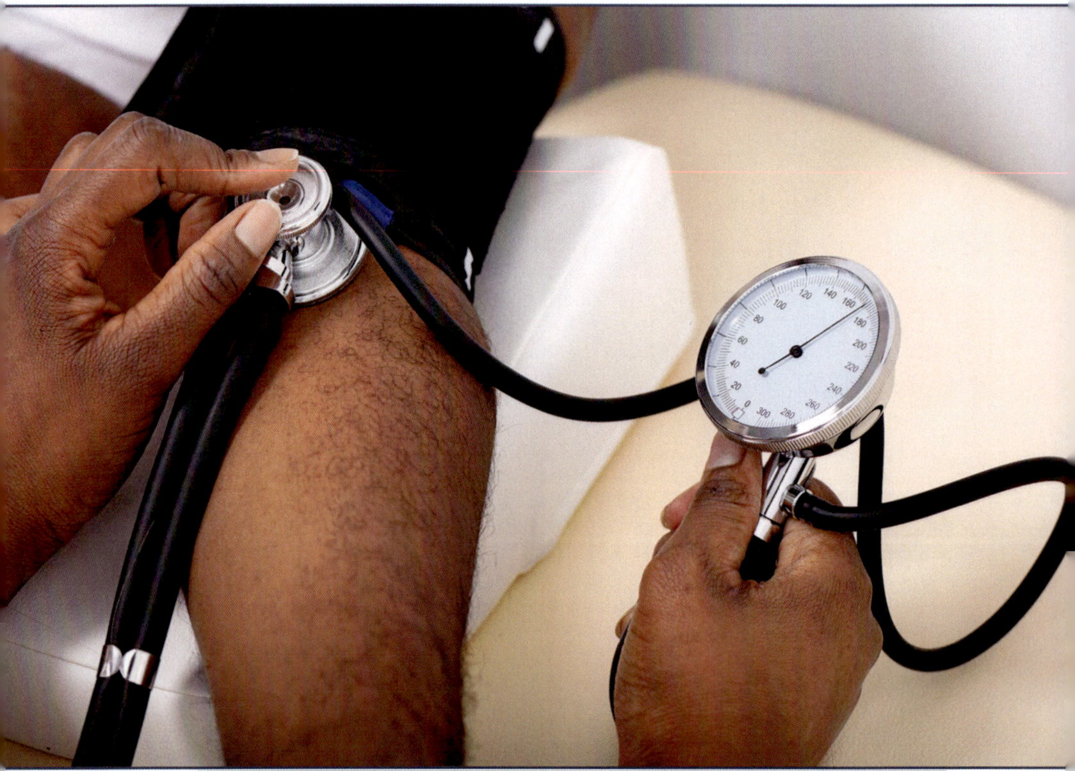

To Jemison, having a stethoscope symbolized being a doctor. A stethoscope amplifies the sounds taking place inside the body of a human or animal, including heart and lung sounds.

cheaper bag instead. The only thing that was difficult for Jemison was learning how to ask people to take off their clothes so that she could examine them naked. She managed to make it comfortable for the patient, but she remained embarrassed!

Working in Africa

In the summer between her second and third years of medical school, Jemison went to Kenya, a country in Africa. Going to Kenya seemed to bring together many of Jemison's interests, such as African culture, medicine, and helping others. She went there on a grant from the International Travelers Association. Although she had fun going to game parks, places where people can see wild animals in their natural habitat, Jemison also worked hard. She assisted the Flying Doctors, a part of the African Medical and Research Foundation (AMREF). This group of doctors and other Western health care professionals went into little-traveled areas of East Africa to provide medical care and health services, even including surgery, to people who had none of those services or care. Jemison did community health service work for this group, walking door to door

AMREF employed a community health worker to show these Maasai young mothers in Kenya how to use a condom and other contraceptives.

in villages and measuring the health of the people, recording the height and weight of the children, and seeing how many of these people were vaccinated for certain diseases. She also assisted with surgery and worked in a hospital and clinic.

As always with Jemison, she managed to have a lot of fun while working hard. Nairobi, the capital city of Kenya, had movie theaters, and Jemison managed to see *Moonraker*, a James Bond movie, in one of them. She also enjoyed some more mundane everyday activities, such as going to the hair salon. It was a big kick for her to be able to walk into any hair salon and have her hair done right, which didn't always happen in America. Most important, she liked the sense of belonging that she felt being among Africans.

After eight weeks of living and working in Kenya, she traveled to Egypt and Israel. She had two weeks to do all of this traveling before she had to get back to her third year of medical school. In Egypt, Jemison saw the pyramids, Luxor Temple, and the Nile. She even saw King Tut's tomb. In Israel, she stayed on a kibbutz with a woman she'd met on the plane coming into Israel.

When she got back to Cornell, she began doing medical rotations. Students doing rotations stayed up for thirty-six hours straight, checking on patients in hospitals. The experience taught her that she could still be effective and think clearly after many hours with no sleep.

Jemison had enjoyed her experience in Kenya greatly. For that reason, she seized the opportunity

This 1979 photo shows Cambodian refugees in Thailand. The refugees are waiting to see doctors at a temporary camp. Many of the refugees arrived there weak from lack of food.

to spend the summer between her third and fourth years of medical school in a refugee camp in Thailand. Refugees are people who flee their country because it is dangerous. They seek a safe place in another, more peaceful, country. Many Cambodians had fled from the war in their country to Thailand. Jemison helped them recover from their health problems, such as malnutrition, tuberculosis (a lung ailment), and dysentery (a disease marked by severe diarrhea usually caused by bacteria in contaminated water).

After finishing medical school, she had a degree in medicine. That did not mean that she could practice medicine; for that, she needed a license. And to get a license, she needed to complete an internship and a board examination. Most doctors also complete a residency, which gives new doctors experience in specialized areas of medicine, such as obstetrics or pediatrics. Jemison had never intended to practice medicine, so she wasn't sure that she wanted to get into a residency program. In such a program, new doctors get paid very little and work about eighty hours a week, learning the ropes from experienced doctors. She had graduated from medical school. What would she do next?

CHAPTER FOUR

SERVING HER COUNTRY

After she graduated medical school, Jemison figured that the best way to ensure that she would get back to pursuing her interest in practicing medicine in developing countries was simple: she would take a one-year internship, with nothing planned after it. She figured that having nothing planned would force her to pursue her dream of working in a developing country, instead of going into a residency program in the United States. Usually, students planned their residencies after their internship, but Jemison did not, even though her professors tried to convince her that she was making a mistake. During a residency, young doctors work a lot of hours under the supervision of more experienced doctors to learn a wide variety of specialized branches of medicine. But Jemison's objectives were clear to her. She wanted to work in developing countries for a while, then go on to do graduate work in engineering, specifically doing biomedical engineering research.

Jemison did her internship year in Los Angeles at the Los Angeles County/University of Southern California Medical Center (LAC/USC). She spent the year as a general practitioner, which means that she did not specialize in one area of medicine, but treated everyone from babies to the elderly. During this time, she was still looking for ways that she could practice medicine in developing countries. She applied to many organizations, writing that she could work as either a physician or an engineer, whichever they needed her to be. Eventually, the Peace Corps offered her a position in West Africa.

Life in the Peace Corps

From 1983 to 1985, Jemison was with the Peace Corps in West Africa. The Peace Corps is an organization that was started in 1961 by President John F. Kennedy. The organization's mission is to

President John F. Kennedy signs the 1961 Peace Corps Bill in the White House. As of September 2018, more than 235,000 Americans have served in the Peace Corps.

send volunteers to developing countries in Africa, Asia, South America, and anywhere else they are needed. The volunteers help the citizens of those countries in whatever area they need help, such as in health care, agriculture, and education. Sometimes the volunteers help to set up better school systems or health care clinics. Sometimes the volunteers help people learn more efficient ways of growing food.

Jemison served as the area Peace Corps medical officer for Sierra Leone and Liberia. That means she was the general manager for the Peace Corps' health care system in those two areas. What does a general manager do? Mae Jemison was only twenty-six years old, and she was responsible for taking care of the health of all the US Peace Corps volunteers, staff members, embassy personnel of Sierra Leone, and the Peace Corps volunteers in Liberia. She managed a medical office, a laboratory, a pharmacy, and volunteer health training. She was also the primary care doctor, which meant that everybody went to her first before being assigned to another doctor. All of the volunteers came to her for their assignments, too. She was on call twenty-four hours a day, seven days a week, for two and a half years.

During her time in West Africa, Mae Jemison treated diseases that she had only read about in textbooks. She worked with some of the best doctors and nurses in Sierra Leone. The medical equipment

While at the 2018 Beyond Innovation Summit in Santa Clara, California, Jemison was reunited with Dan Anisman, whose life she saved while in Africa thirty years prior.

was, at times, barely adequate for their purposes. It was always a challenge to get the supplies and the equipment needed. While she was working in Sierra Leone, Jemison not only helped others as a doctor, she tried to help them take care of their own health. She wrote manuals for self-care. She wrote and enforced guidelines for public health and safety. She did research on a hepatitis B vaccine, rabies, and schistosomiasis, an illness that you can get from any one of five species of waterborne flatworms called schistosomes. The parasite can also be found in snails, which is why the disease is sometimes called snail fever. She did this work with the help of two prestigious American health organizations, the National Institutes of Health (NIH) and the Centers for Disease Control and Prevention (CDC).

Jemison was proud of the work that she did in Africa. According to *Black Explorers* by Catherine Reef, she said, "I was doing work that affected people's lives and whether they lived or died. I learned to trust myself and work with myself and develop the confidence that I'm able to take care of things on my own."

Jemison returned to Los Angeles in the summer of 1985. She spent two years working as a general practitioner at Cigna health plans of California.

The Space Age

President John F. Kennedy gave a historic speech to Congress in which he said:

> *I believe that this nation should commit itself to achieving the goal, before this decade is out, of landing a man on the moon and returning him safely to the Earth. No single space project in this period will be more impressive to mankind, or more important for the long-range exploration of space; and none will be so difficult or expensive to accomplish.*

The space race, as it was called, did not come out of nowhere. It was a response by the United States to the advances in space exploration made by the Soviet Union. The Soviet Union had launched ***Sputnik 1***, the first space capsule, in October 1957. A few weeks later, ***Sputnik 2*** was launched, with a dog named Laika aboard. That was the first space capsule that was launched with a living thing onboard. The United States did not launch space capsules until 1958. President Kennedy, who became president in 1961, devoted much time and effort to funding America's space program.

Yuri A. Gagarin became the first human to go into space in April 1961. In ***Vostok 1***, he orbited Earth for almost two hours. In February 1962, John Glenn became the first American in space. He orbited Earth three times in ***Friendship 7***.

Entering NASA

Jemison applied to NASA, the National Aeronautics and Space Administration, in 1985. She had had an interest in space and a desire to be an astronaut since she was a girl. Before NASA officials had a chance to review her application, the space shuttle *Challenger* blew up on January 28, 1986, just seventy-three seconds after liftoff. All seven crew members were killed, including Christa McAuliffe, a high school teacher from New Hampshire, and Ronald McNair, an African American astronaut. It was unclear whether there would be a space shuttle program at all after this tragedy. NASA stopped the next fourteen shuttle missions, saying that they would be rescheduled when scientists learned why such an accident had happened. They also wanted to learn how they could prevent something like that from ever happening again. Mae Jemison, although she was as shocked and sad as anyone else was about what had happened to the crew members of the *Challenger*, reapplied to NASA when the space shuttle missions were resumed.

Jemison was ecstatic when she got a call asking her if she could come to the Johnson Space Center

This official portrait shows the STS-51L mission crewmembers, who lost their lives on January 28, 1986, when the space shuttle they were in, *Challenger*, exploded during launch.

(JSC) in Houston, Texas, for interviews. Out of the two thousand people who had applied to the space shuttle program, NASA interviewed about one hundred of them, and Mae Jemison was going to be one of them. She desperately wanted to go, but she worried about how to get the time off from her work at Cigna without anyone knowing where she had gone. All of her life, people had given her mixed signals about her desire to be an astronaut. Her parents were always supportive, but Jemison could never tell whether they really believed in her dream or if they were just humoring her. Others were downright negative about her chances for success in the astronaut program. Jemison decided to keep the interview a secret until she found out whether she had been chosen or not. She told only the office manager because she needed to get time off from work. In her autobiography, Jemison wrote, "Believe it or not, I was as excited or more so when called for the astronaut interview than when I was selected. Why? Because, I had looked good on paper! My college and medical school transcripts that I fretted over were fine."

An Important Interview

Always one to be prepared, Jemison read books about the history of space exploration before she went to her interview at the Johnson Space Center in Houston, Texas. Astronaut interviews take one week. Medical exams and checkups are given to make sure that the candidates are perfectly healthy. Being in space is an abnormal environment for the human body to be in. Therefore, NASA wants to make sure that astronauts are in the healthiest condition that they can be in before they get placed into the abnormal, stressful environment of outer space. Astronauts can't have any chronic illnesses, such as diabetes, or any physiologic abnormalities, like heart arrhythmia, a condition that means your heartbeat is irregular. Those interviewing to become astronauts take eye exams to test their eyesight, blood tests, muscle strength tests, hearing tests, and psychological tests. Jemison wrote in her autobiography:

> *A personal favorite was an isolation/claustrophobia test where I was asked to sit inside a three-foot-diameter balloon with air blowing in it for thirty minutes. I got in and started to hum and sing to myself, then fell asleep. The operator said I was the first one he had seen do that.*

However, not everything went perfectly smoothly for Jemison during her interview. One of her physical checkups showed that she had a heart murmur. Sometimes having a heart murmur means that there is something wrong with your heart, but sometimes a murmur is just a murmur and there is nothing wrong with the heart. Jemison explained to the doctor that she knew all about the heart murmur. When she was in medical school, a doctor told her about it. He also told her it was called a functional flow murmur, which meant that there was nothing wrong with her heart. Jemison had to get a special heart test called an echocardiogram to see whether her heart was okay. She was relieved to find out that it was fine and that she was still in the running to be an astronaut.

CHAPTER FIVE

MAKING THE GRADE IN SPACE

Despite Jemison's attempts at secrecy, everyone at work quickly found out about her trip to NASA. Several of her friends reported that the FBI had questioned them about her, a routine part of background investigations for astronauts. Jemison also talked with the FBI. Business continued as usual. Jemison worked at Cigna during the day and took graduate classes in engineering and business at UCLA at night.

One day in June 1987, she got the call that she had been selected as an astronaut. She had been one of the fifteen people chosen out of about two thousand applicants. She was asked not to tell anyone until the next day, when a press release would be broadcast on television news and in newspapers, announcing who had been selected to the astronaut program. It was difficult for Jemison not to tell anyone; she just had to call her parents and tell them. She also told her cat, Sneeze, whom she had gotten as a little kitten in Sierra Leone. According to her autobiography, "I told Sneeze we were moving to Houston. He was completely cool with it."

Intensive Training

There is a long process between getting accepted into NASA's astronaut training program and actually becoming an astronaut. There are many different parts of the training, which lasts for about a year but can take longer, depending on the mission for which candidates are being groomed. Astronauts must be physically healthy, but they must also be psychologically and emotionally healthy. NASA also wants well-rounded people who can work well with others but who have the strength of personality to be able to make good decisions if they have to. According to *And Not Afraid to Dare* by Tonya Bolden, a book

Jemison trains in parachute survival school for a weeklong flight scheduled for June 1991. The mission included experiments in life sciences and materials processing.

that explores the lives of ten inspirational African American women, "Astronauts are expected to be team players and highly skilled generalists with just the right amount of individuality and self-reliance to be effective crew members."

Astronauts are trained to make sure that they know everything they need to know while they are onboard a spacecraft. The first thing that has to be done with the new members of NASA is to make sure that everyone has the same common starting point of knowledge about spaceflight. The class of new astronauts in which Mae Jemison found herself came from a variety of different backgrounds, including a meteorologist (a scientist who studies weather), a mechanical engineer, and herself, a medical doctor. The class studied many subjects, such as oceanography, navigation, mathematics, and astronomy.

The class also did some hands-on training outside of the classroom. This included parachute training and survival training on supersonic aircraft. They had to learn this because astronauts use supersonic aircraft in emergency situations. They also did scuba diving and land-and-sea survival training. This is important because astronauts need to be prepared for whatever happens. Of course no one at NASA plans for a spacecraft to make an emergency landing in the middle of the ocean, but mistakes can happen. Astronauts learn what to do in any emergency.

The class also learned all about spacecraft and how to be in orbit. They learned about weightlessness, which is what happens when the human body gets into outer space and escapes gravity. Gravity is what holds us down. When there is no gravity, the body experiences weightlessness—it floats. The class learned about the history and dangers of spaceflight and what had happened to cause the *Challenger* accident. They learned about every part of a space shuttle, as well as about planets, weather patterns, and geology.

What Does a Mission Specialist Do?

Jemison would be the mission specialist on the spaceflight. That meant that she was not expected to learn how to fly the supersonic aircraft. She just had to know how to handle the radios, how to fly straight, how to follow headings and flight courses, how to control the aircraft when it was off the ground, and how to plan the flight. She would have many responsibilities. She had to do work to make sure the craft ran well. She might also be taking space walks. But the main task was to oversee and to participate in the many scientific experiments that would be done aboard her ship, the *Endeavour*.

In August 1988, at the end of her training, Mae Jemison became an astronaut. All she had to do was wait for a mission. While the astronauts were waiting for a mission, they continued to train. Those who were selected to be on the *Endeavour* trained for two years, much of the time in Japan, to learn about the experiments they would be conducting when the *Endeavour* went into orbit. In Japan, they met and trained with Dr. Mamoru Mohri, who would be on the crew of the *Endeavour*. He was the first Japanese national to fly in a space shuttle.

To Go Where No One Has Gone Before

Mae Jemison had never given up her love of science fiction. So when she had the opportunity to meet Nichelle Nichols, the actress who played the character

(continued on p. 71)

Jemison (*left*) helps actress Nichelle Nichols (*right*) celebrate her eighty-fifth birthday during a party held in Los Angeles on December 28, 2017.

(continued from p. 69)

Lieutenant Uhuru on the original ***Star Trek*** series, which ran from 1963 to 1966.

Jemison is a huge ***Star Trek*** fan, and Nichols was doing a ***Star Trek*** convention in Florida, near the Kennedy Space Center. Jemison sought out Nichols there. When Nichols heard who was standing outside her dressing room door, she insisted that Jemison be brought in immediately. Nichols gave Jemison a warm hug, and the two have been friends ever since.

In fact, Jemison appeared on an episode of ***Star Trek: The Next Generation,*** which aired on June 6, 1992. The episode was called "Second Chances," and Jemison played a character called Ensign Palmer.

3 ... 2 ... 1 ... Liftoff!

Mae C. Jemison was thirty-six years old when she boarded the *Endeavour* on September 12, 1992. The *Endeavour* had been built to replace the *Challenger*, and this was the *Endeavour*'s second flight. The six other astronauts on the *Endeavour* were Robert L. "Hoot" Gibson, Curtis L. Brown, Mark C. Lee, Mamoru Mohri, Jerome "Jay" Apt, and N. Jan Davis. The *Endeavour* mission was important for many reasons and made quite a few firsts. In addition to

Jemison being the first African American woman astronaut, the *Endeavour* mission was the first time that a married couple—Lee and Davis—would go on a mission together. It was also the first time that a mission science specialist would be aboard a spacecraft, and it was the first joint mission between the United States and Japan.

Before the launch at the Kennedy Space Center at Cape Canaveral, Florida, Jemison helped to get the space shuttle ready for the launch. She had to make sure that the thermal protection system was working properly. This system is composed of tiles on the outside of the shuttle that shield the spacecraft from heat when it reenters Earth's atmosphere. The reentry makes so much heat that without the thermal protection system, the spacecraft would burn up.

The flight was called the STS-47 Spacelab J. Jemison knew that it was not only a fulfillment of her lifelong dream, but that her achievement was a symbol for many people. According to Reef's *Black Explorers*, Jemison said, "It was the realization of many dreams of many people." In her interviews with the press, Jemison made it very clear that, although she was the first African American female astronaut, she was not the only African American astronaut at NASA. There were six others.

High Above the Earth

Jemison brought into space with her some items that had personal significance. She carried a poster of the Alvin Ailey dance troupe, from the dance production "Cry," which was specifically about African American women's struggles and achievements. She carried a flag from the Organization of African Unity, and a banner from the Mae C. Jemison Academy in Detroit, Michigan—an alternate public school established in 1992 to teach science and mathematics to children in preschool classes through the second grade. Some people criticized her choice of items to bring aboard, saying that she should have brought things that represented all people and not just African Americans. However, Mae Jemison had not had an easy road to get to be aboard the *Endeavour*, and it was important to her to bring objects that represented not only her struggle, but the struggle of her people, particularly African American women. She told Constance M. Green in an interview for *Ms.* magazine:

The crew of STS-47 poses aboard the space shuttle *Endeavour*. Jemison (*far right*) and her fellow astronauts spent eight days in space in 1992.

When I'm asked about the relevance to black people of what I do, I take that as an affront. It presupposes that black people have never been involved in exploring the heavens, but that is not so. Ancient African empires—Mali, Songhay, Egypt—had scientists, astronomers. The fact is that space and its resources belong to all of us, not to any one group.

Part of Jemison's duties was to make the space shuttle into the laboratory they would need to conduct experiments. Jemison was part of the blue shift, which was basically the night shift. The red shift was the day shift. Jan Davis and Jay Apt worked with Jemison on the blue shift. The scientists conducted more than forty-four experiments, designed by scientists from across the United States and Japan. Some of these scientists worked for NASA and for NASDA, the Japanese Space Agency. Some were from universities or corporations.

They studied how the human body operates in weightlessness and how it responds to being in zero gravity. Jemison designed an experiment to study the effect of space travel on human bone cells. Astronauts can lose calcium from being in weightlessness a long time. The crew also did experiments with frogs' eggs to see whether fertilized frogs' eggs can develop into tadpoles in zero gravity. During the spaceflight, the astronauts talked by radio with schoolchildren all over the world. Jemison talked with kids in her hometown of Chicago.

The *Endeavour* landed after eight days in orbit. The city of Chicago held a six-day celebration in

In this 1992 photo, Jemison (*right*) sits next to Earl Bryant (*left*), principal of her alma mater Morgan Park High School, during a ceremony to honor her achievements as an astronaut.

honor of Mae Jemison, the first African American female astronaut. The celebration took place on her thirty-sixth birthday on October 17, 1992. Jemison had been an astronaut for six years, but only six months after her space shuttle flight, Jemison resigned from NASA. According to *Black*

Explorers, she said, "I leave with the honor of having been the first woman of color in space and with an appreciation of NASA—the organization that gave me the opportunity to make one of my dreams possible."

In her autobiography, she wrote, "Looking down and all around me, seeing the earth, the moon, and the stars, I felt just like I belonged right here, and in fact, any place in the entire universe."

Mae Jemison had achieved her dream of going into space. What would she do once she had her feet on the ground again?

CHAPTER SIX

LEAVING NASA

After all the training and anticipation of the *Endeavour* mission was finished, Jemison resigned from NASA just six months later. She weathered criticism for that decision from some who accused her of seeking fame instead of being committed to space technology.

Jemison, though, wanted to get back to her goals of helping developing countries and teaching young people. In January 1993, Mae Jemison accepted a teaching position at Dartmouth College in New Hampshire. She taught a course about space-age technology in developing countries. She continued to teach at Dartmouth for six years. Jemison also found time to devote her knowledge and experience

Jemison (*right*) speaks with Jill Giovanelli (*left*) after a 1994 United Nations' ceremony in which Giovanelli's peace poster won a worldwide poster competition.

to various organizations that bear her name.

Private Enterprise

When Jemison left NASA in 1993, she founded the Jemison Group, Inc., a company that focuses on projects that combine social science issues with science and technology. Some of the projects on which the group has worked include Alafiya, which explores how to speed up and enhance health care in Africa by using a satellite-based telecommunication system. The group has also worked on designing solar-thermal electricity generating systems, which are ways of getting energy by harnessing the power of the sun. In addition to all of this great research, the group has introduced science and literature education into South Africa and has produced 3-D, real-time pilot-in-the-loop simulations for desktop computers, helping pilots learn how to fly aircraft.

Mae Jemison is also the director of the Jemison Institute for Advancing Technology in Developing Countries. It is an organization that researches, designs, and puts into real-life situations the newest scientific technologies.

Giving Back

Jemison started the Dorothy Jemison Foundation for Excellence (DJF) to honor her mother, Dorothy Jemison. DJF is a nonprofit organization. The organization runs on funds that various people and other organizations, including the government, provide. Organized to help schools and teachers make science more fun and challenging for the students, DJF does this by emphasizing hands-on experiments. Such activities are more fun than sitting in a classroom listening to a teacher talk about science. DJF also encourages students to think about applying what they learn in science to benefit the world; that is, making a social contribution using scientific study.

High school student Mary King (*left*) and Mae Jemison (*right*) help Angie Hancock (*center*) to perform a science experiment during Angie's stay at Children's Hospital in Denver.

The goals of the foundation are modeled after the teaching principles and life accomplishments of Dorothy Mae Jemison. Dorothy Jemison taught for more than twenty-five years in the Chicago public school system. Her personal formula for excellence can be seen not only in her teaching career, but in the success of her three children, who all went on to become successful members of society. Ada is a child psychiatrist and Charles is a real estate broker. A major project of the Dorothy Jemison Foundation is The Earth We Share (TEWS).

The Earth We Share

The Earth We Share is an international science camp, of which Jemison is the director. The mission of the camp is to provide meaningful experiences in the sciences for teens. Jemison herself developed many of the programs and experiments conducted at the camp, and she works directly with the campers. Classes are held at colleges in the United States, such as Dartmouth College in New Hampshire and Talladega College in Alabama. Camp lasts for four weeks each summer.

During that time, kids from all over the United States and countries around the world work with teachers and interns in teams of eight to ten students. The teams apply critical-thinking skills to provide solutions to the problems that affect us globally. These problems could be anything from what to

Jemison accompanied two other retired astronauts to Shanghai, China, in 2005 to deliver a speech at DuPont research center.

do about the greenhouse effect to how to solve the overpopulation problem. Some of the topics have included the following: Ways to determine if there is life elsewhere in the universe (and whether this life is intelligent life); predicting the hot public stocks of the year 2030; designing a crime control system for the year 2005; mapping out the world's perfect house; and coming up with an exercise program to keep high school students healthy. The teams create ideas about how to solve the problems. Then they create experiments in which they test their hypotheses. When the experiments are finished, kids evaluate the results of what they've done. In this way, they can see how successful they've been at helping to solve world problems. Each topic requires the application of physics, mathematics, chemistry, biology, environmental sciences, and the social sciences.

Making Science Make Sense

Since 1995, Jemison has served as the national science literacy advocate for Bayer Corporation and its Making Science Make Sense program. Making Science Make Sense supports hands-on science

Honors and Awards

Throughout the years, Jemison has been granted many honors. Some were given to her to recognize her hard work and contributions to society. Other awards were simply to acknowledge her selflessness and beauty, both inside and out.

Jemison was selected as one of the nation's top seven women leaders in a poll conducted by the White House in January 1999; she was awarded the Kilby Science Award in 1993; she was inducted into the National Women's Hall of Fame in 1993; Johnson Publications gave her the Black Achievement Trailblazers Award in 1992; ***McCall's*** magazine named her one of 10 Outstanding Women for the '90s in 1991. Jemison also holds numerous honorary doctoral degrees. She was even named one of ***People*** magazine's World's 50 Most Beautiful People in 1993, for her stunning good looks.

learning in schools and helps ordinary citizens to understand how scientific studies can help benefit our planet and our quality of life.

Being an advocate means that Jemison speaks in support of science literacy, or helping people have an easier time studying and reading about scientific subjects. Jemison travels with Bayer executives around the country, encouraging teachers and school system officials to provide quality hands-on science education that stimulates students to think critically. She has visited about two dozen cities, meeting with thousands of people, including principals and school district administrators; federal, state, and local government officials; community leaders; and parents, teachers, and students.

A Life of Exploration

Apart from being the recipient of numerous awards from the media and the scientific community, Jemison was the subject of a PBS documentary, called *The New Explorers*. She also hosted and served as the technical consultant on *World of Wonder*, a weekly television program that aired on the Discovery Channel from 1994 to 1995. Jemison serves on the board of directors of Scholastic, Inc., a children's book publishing company; the Aspen Institute, a nonprofit organization devoted to giving world leaders the tools to improve quality of life; the Keystone Center, a nonprofit organization

Mae Jemison served as the keynote speaker at the Santa Clara, California, Beyond Innovation Summit held on May 23, 2018.

whose aim is to improve science education by introducing hands-on projects; the National Urban League, a nationwide organization that spreads information on civil rights and racial equality; and Spelman College, an all-women's, historically black college in Atlanta, Georgia.

In 2018, Jemison promoted the cell phone technology space helped create by participating in an app called Skyfie (in place of selfie) designed to interest people worldwide in the sky above them. The app encourages users to capture what they see and feel when they look at the sky by taking videos, photos, audio recordings, or submitting text. These submissions are combined to create a worldwide Sky Tapestry to be shared by all.

Mae Jemison has been a dancer, an astronaut, a doctor, a scientist, and a teacher.

Having achieved her dream of going into space, Mae Jemison has spent her time since her *Endeavour* mission trying to make planet Earth a better place for everyone on it. What does she have in mind for the next step of her fabulous career? In an interview conducted by Kristen Dorsey of the *Virginian-Pilot*, then forty-five-year-old Jemison said, "I'm still deciding what I want to be when I grow up next year."

Timeline

1956 Mae Jemison is born October 17, in Decatur, Alabama.

1972 Mae graduates from high school at the age of sixteen and heads to Stanford University in California.

1977 Jemison receives a BS in chemical engineering and qualifies for a BA in African and Afro-American studies from Stanford University.

1981 Jemison graduates from Cornell University medical school in New York City.

1982 Jemison completes a one-year medical internship at the Los Angeles County/University of Southern California Medical Center.

1983 Jemison spends two years working as a Peace Corps medical officer in Sierra Leone and Liberia, West Africa, overseeing the health care for all Peace Corps workers in those two areas. While there, she also does medical research, writes self-care manuals, and serves as a general practitioner.

1987 NASA accepts Jemison into their astronaut program after a rigorous application and interview process.

1991 *McCall's* magazine names Jemison one of 10 Outstanding Women for the '90s.

1992 On September 12, the *Endeavour* is launched, with Jemison as the mission specialist aboard the spacecraft. Jemison becomes the first African American woman in space. Jemison is awarded the

Kilby Science Award. That same year, she is inducted into the National Women's Hall of Fame in Seneca Falls, New York.

1994 Jemison serves as a Discovery Channel technical consultant for the television program *World of Wonder*.

1995 Jemison begins working with the Bayer Corporation and its Making Science Make Sense program as the national science literacy advocate.

2001 Jemison's autobiography, *Find Where the Wind Goes: Moments from My Life*, is published.

2018 Jemison helps develop an app called Skyfie to build a worldwide tapestry of sky images.

Glossary

antibodies Chemicals that the body makes to fight disease.

bionic Relating to the branch of science that seeks to enhance biological function with the help of electronics or mechanics.

cadaver A human corpse.

claustrophobia The fear of being in small, enclosed spaces.

diorama A small model of something.

dysentery A disease that is marked by dehydration due to severe diarrhea.

evolution How something changed over time or came into being.

grant A sum of money given to someone to help pay for his or her education or study.

hematology A science that deals with the blood.

hypothesis A guess at the outcome of a study.

integrated A term meaning that there is no separation of people of different races.

internship A period of work or study during which students learn more about a chosen career.

kibbutz A farming community in which all members of the community work and share equally.

malnutrition When the body is not getting enough of the vital nutrients it needs to maintain health.

militant Aggressive; engaged in combat.

obstetrics A branch of medicine having to do with childbirth.

pediatrics A branch of medicine having to do with children.

physiology The study of the human body's systems.

satellite A man-made object put into outer space to deliver information to scientists on the ground.

supersonic Faster than the speed of light.

vaccine A substance that is given to people to protect them from a certain disease.

For More Information

Canadian Coalition of Women in Engineering, Science, Trades and Technology (CCWESTT)
c/o Treeline Associates Inc.
1568 Merivale Road, Suite 739
Ottawa, ON K2G 5Y7
Canada
Email: info@ccwestt.org
Website: http://www.ccwestt.org
Facebook and Twitter: @CCWESTT
This nonprofit organization, established in 1992, seeks to bring organizations across Canada together to encourage women in science, technology, engineering, and mathematics (STEM) education and careers.

Centers for Disease Control and Prevention (CDC)
(800) CDC-INFO (800-232-4636)
Website: https://www.cdc.gov
Facebook: @CDC
Twitter and Instagram: @CDCgov
The website provides a wealth of information, from diseases and conditions to healthy living and emergency preparedness.

Dr.Mae.com
Email: info@drmae.com
Website: http://www.maejemison.com
Facebook: @100YearStarship
Twitter: @maejemison
Mae Jemison's official website shares information about Jemison herself and projects she supports such as The Earth We Share (TEWS) and The Dorothy Jemison Foundation for Excellence.

National Aeronautics and Space Administration (NASA)
300 E. Street SW, Suite 5R30
Washington, DC 20546
(202) 358-0001
Website: http://www.nasa.gov
Facebook, Twitter, and Instagram: @NASA
NASA's huge website offers information on various missions, images from space, downloads of apps, podcasts, ebooks, and more.

National Women's Hall of Fame
76 Fall Street
PO Box 335
Seneca Falls, NY 13148

(315) 568-8060
Website: https://www.womenofthehall.org
Twitter and Instagram: @WomenoftheHall
The organization honors and celebrates the achievements of special American women. The website hosts the biographies of numerous celebrated women from the past and present.

Peace Corps
1111 20th Street NW
Washington, DC 20526
(855) 855-1961
Website: http://www.peacecorps.gov
Facebook, Twitter, and Instagram: @peacecorps
The mission of this organization is to promote world peace through serving areas of need while promoting a better understanding of Americans and helping Americans better understand world cultures.

Society for Canadian Women in Science and Technology
#311 – 525 Seymour Street
Vancouver, BC V6B 3H7
Canada

(604) 893-8657
Email: resourcecentre@scwist.ca
Website: http://www.scwist.ca
Twitter: @scwist
This nonprofit organization is dedicated to promoting and empowering girls and women in science, engineering, and technology.

Women's International Center (WIC)
PO Box 880736
San Diego, CA 92168-0736
(619) 295-6446
Website: http://www.wic.org
Facebook: @https://www.facebook.com/Womens-International-Center-and-Living-Legacy-Awards-106237102802079/
Dedicated to celebrating the accomplishments of women worldwide, WIC's website offers biographies of hundreds of important women creators, workers, and dignitaries.

For Further Reading

Brererton, Catherine. *Women Scientists in Math and Coding*. Mankato, MN: Core Library, 2017.

Gagne, Tammy. *Women in Engineering*. Mankato, MN: Core Library, 2017.

Gagne, Tammy. *Women in Medicine*. Mankato, MN: Core Library, 2017.

Halligan, Katherine. *HerStory: 50 Women and Girls Who Shook Up the World*. New York, NY: Simon & Schuster Books for Young Readers, 2018.

Jackson, Libby. *Galaxy Girls: 50 Amazing Stories of Women in Space*. New York, NY: Harper Design, 2017.

Jemison, Mae. *Find Where the Wind Goes: Moments from My Life*. New York, NY: Scholastic, Inc., 2001.

Mangor, Jodie. *Women in Physical Science*. New York, NY: Enslow Publishers, 2017.

Ploscariu, Iemima. *Mae Carol Jemison: Astronaut and Educator.* Minneapolis, MN: Essential Library, 2018.

Randolph, Joanne. *African American Inventors & Scientists*. New York, NY: Enslow Publishers, 2018.

Schmermund, Elizabeth. *Women in Technology*. New York, NY: Enslow Publishers, 2017.

Bibliography

Bolden, Tonya. *And Not Afraid to Dare*. New York, NY: Scholastic, Inc., 1998.

Dorothy Jemison Foundation for Excellence. "Sky Tapestry." Retrieved on April 7, 2019. https://lookuponesky.com/sky-tapestry.

Dorsey, Kristen. "Ex-Astronaut Wants to Help Youths Launch Their Futures." *The Virginian-Pilot*, February 22, 2002.

"Dr. Mae Jemison." Retrieved February 11, 2019. https://starchild.gsfc.nasa.gov/docs/StarChild/whos_who_level2/jemison.html.

Encyclopedia of World Biography. "Mae Jemison Biography - Life, Family, Childhood, Children, Parents, School, Young, Information, Born, College." Retrieved February 11, 2019. https://www.notablebiographies.com/Ho-Jo/Jemison-Mae.html.

Jemison, Mae. *Find Where the Wind Goes: Moments from My Life*. New York, NY: Scholastic, Inc., 2001.

KDCAH – Katherine Dunham Centers for Arts and Humanities. "Katherine Dunham Biography (1909–2006)." Retrieved April 7, 2019. http://kdcah.org/katherine-dunham-biography.

Phelps, J. Alfred. *They Had a Dream: The Story of African-American Astronauts*. Novato, CA: Presidio, 1994.

Reef, Catherine. *Black Explorers*. New York, NY: Facts on File, 1996.

Space.com Staff. "May 25, 1961: JFK's Moon Shot Speech to Congress." May 25, 2011. https://www.space.com/11772-president-kennedy-historic-speech-moon-space.html.

Index

G

H

I

J

K

L

M

About the Authors

Xina M. Uhl is the author of numerous books, lessons, and assessment questions in the educational field. A graduate of Arizona State University (BA) and California State University Northridge (MA), she enjoys reading and researching at every opportunity. Learn about her fiction on her blog.

Magdalena Alagna is an editor and freelance writer living in New York City.

Photo Credits

Cover, pp. 5, 60, 74 NASA; p. 9 Leadinglights/iStock Unreleased /Getty Images; p. 14 Bruce Leighty/Photolibrary/Getty Images; p. 16 Barry Philp/Toronto Star/Getty Images; p. 21 BSIP/UIG /Getty Images; p. 24 Seth Poppel/Yearbook Library; p. 30 Stanford News Service; p. 32 Edson Campolina/Shutterstock.com; p. 34 Michael Ochs Archives/Getty Images; p. 39 The Washington Post /Getty Images; p. 42 John D. Kisch/Separate Cinema Archive/Archive Photos/Getty Images; p. 46 Andrey_Popov/Shutterstock.com; p. 48 Jonathan Torgovnik/Getty Images; p. 50 Bettmann /Getty Images; p. 54 PhotoQuest/Archive Photos/Getty Images; pp. 56, 87 Lachlan Cunningham/Getty Images; pp. 66, 76, 79 © AP Images; p. 70 Albert L. Ortega/Getty Images; p. 81 Lyn Alweis /The Denver Post/Getty Images; p. 83 China Photos/Getty Images; halftone circle graphics shumbrat/Shutterstock.com; rainbow zigzag graphics pro500/Shutterstock.com.

Design and Layout: Nicole Russo-Duca; Photo Researcher: Nicole DiMella